44 Easy Online Business Ideas You Can Start Now:online business thoughts that could make you rich

JAMES S.GRIEGO

44 Easy Online Business Ideas You Can Start Now

Numerous of the items included here are all from our accomplices who repay us. This might impact which items we expound on and where and how the item shows up on a page. In any case, this doesn't impact our assessments. Our perspectives are our own. Here is a rundown of our accomplices and this is the way we bring in cash.

For some future business people, maintaining a web-based business is a fantasy that offers the commitment of monetary security and freedom. To assist you with starting the most common way of beginning your own internet-based business and acquiring the adaptability and opportunity that accompanies it, we've incorporated this rundown of the best web-based independent venture thoughts. None of these web-based business thoughts require an actual customer-facing facade and for certain thoughts, so you don't bring to the table for an actual item, simply a help.

Also, if you're telecommuting you can decide your schedule, work for yourself and guarantee workspace charge derivations. Thus, assuming you're prepared to get everything rolling on your fantasy about turning into a web business person, begin with this rundown of online business thoughts for amateurs and track down the one that best accommodates your abilities and interests.

The 44 best internet-based business thoughts
With the enormous development of the web and innovation, by and large, there's an internet-based business thought out there for everybody, no matter what your experience or earlier work history. Beginning a web-based business can be one of the speediest, simplest, and most reasonable ways of beginning a business in

general — particularly when all you want is a PC and web association.

As telecommuting has become more well-known in organizational societies all over the planet, business people have been roused to assume control over their vocations and start a new business for themselves. Furthermore, on the off chance that you're not completely set on betting everything on your internet-based business, a considerable lot of these thoughts can be begun part-time, and as you fabricate your side gig, it could find lasting success enough to transform into a full-time gig.

1. Virtual entertainment promoting
If you have a talent for getting likes, top choices, retweets, devotees, offers, remarks, and snaps, then, at that point, you should consider a vocation in web-based entertainment promoting. By talking with organizations to deal with their virtual entertainment profiles, spread their

substance across the Web, keep their brands on target, and answer client questions, you can transform your number one side interest into your normal employment.

2. Web optimization counseling
Perhaps you're a star at SEO or site improvement. On the off chance that you have heaps of expertise and involvement with getting sites to rank profoundly on Google, and you comprehend how to transform searchers into clients, then, at that point, there are a lot of organizations able to pay liberally for your assistance.

Whether it's by altering metadata labels, routinely refreshing the organization's blog, or looking for brilliant catchphrases to rank profoundly on, a decent SEO specialist working with a strong SEO procedure can radically change how an organization's site seems to web search tool clients — and only a couple of positions on Google can have an enormous effect in rush hour gridlock numbers. To put it plainly, you could immensely affect a business' main concern, and that implies this web-based business thought is popular.

The amount Do You Need?

$
with Fundera by NerdWallet
3. Independent planning
Got an eye for style? Did you go to craftsmanship school, or have you generally invest your free energy planning banners in Photoshop or Illustrator?

Provided that this is true, and assuming you're keen on finding the gig on this rundown of online private venture thoughts that is ideal for you, then, at that point, independent planning may be a decent decision. Take on clients at your speed, develop a decent standing on the web, and by listening in on others' conversations and work on projects that you view as fascinating — outsourcing has a lot of advantages.

Look at locales like Upwork and Behance to track down the right gigs to partake in the opportunity of an independent way of life.

4. Independent composition
On the off chance that you're talented in words, all things considered, you could turn into an independent essayist. Insofar as you have a web association and a console, you can contribute blog entries.

It helps if you have an extraordinary area of interest or mastery, so your bosses will realize you're able to remark on specific subjects. Nonetheless, the main element will constantly be your composition. Could you at any point compose obviously? Do you take the time and work to truly comprehend what you're referring to? Might it be said that you are interesting to the right perusers? On the off chance that you're certain about your composing abilities, this internet-based business thought is great.

5. digital book composing

On the off chance that organization blog entries aren't your style, then, at that point, you should seriously think about composition and distributing digital books all things being equal. With Amazon and different sites around, independently publishing has never been simpler than it is today. On the off chance that you think you have something intriguing or valuable to say — and you accept others will suspect as much, as well — then, at that point, composing digital books could turn into a rewarding business.

With digital books, you don't need to configure, print, or boat your work. Simply compose, market, distribute and sell — to anybody on the planet. Furthermore, since you're distributing the book yourself, you get a bigger cut of the benefits when the digital book takes off. You should figure out how to organize a digital book accurately, pay for altering and cover configuration administrations and sort out a viable advertising technique — yet fortunately, there are a lot of guides to gain from.

6. Interpretation

On the off chance that you're an extraordinary essayist yet aren't so keen on distributing unique material, we've got some simple internet-based business thoughts for you. If you're conversant in various dialects, for instance, deciphering could be the best work. You can do it any place you'd like, since you have the text you're chipping away at and you figure out the objective of the interpretation.

7. Altering

Altering comes in many shapes and sizes, from copyediting an organization's showcasing materials to editing books to ordering scholastic compositions. However long you have a sharp eye for detail, areas of strength for language, and a readiness to get in the weeds, then, at that point, altering could be an extraordinary business thought assuming you're keen on working when and how you need.

8. Composing a blog
While a blog isn't precisely a business, it can uphold any of these web-based business thoughts you're browsing.

Independent essayist or fashioner? Flaunt your abilities in each post. Keen on coding, photography and video, wellness, food, or something else? Demonstrate your insight by composing extraordinary articles on those subjects.

The more individuals trust your position, the more they'll peruse, and the more extensive your crowd, the simpler it is to develop your business by publishing content to a blog. Regardless of whether you're choosing which of these internet-based business thoughts to seek after, beginning a blog is never an impractical notion, as you'll lay out a web-based presence to work from.

9. Independent exploring
Independent exploring is another brilliant internet-based business thought that allows you to work from any place, according to your preferences. You needn't bother with being a gifted essayist or a conceived planner, simply dedicated and aware of how to find what you want.

Whether you're assembling research reports for a contender or statistical surveying, responding to intense specialized inquiries on discussions, or examining measurements to bring up patterns, you'll accomplish important work for your clients — and doing it at a decent cost, with the opportunity to work how you need.

10. Independent coding and website architecture

Notice a pattern yet? Heaps of occupations you could be doing in an office for one organization, you could likewise be accomplished for a lot of various clients at whatever point and anyway you need.

If you're a computer programmer, the advantages of working at a startup or tech goliath are sizable, yet on the off chance that you're more put resources into adaptability, variety of tasks, taking on work at your speed and the opportunity of working for yourself, then independent coding is one of the most outstanding web-based business thoughts from home. Whether you're into website composition — a particularly famous independent coding class — or one more sort of programming improvement, it ought not to be an over-the-top test to find clients you're keen on assisting.

Furthermore, you can twofold down as a product specialist too, offering your basic eye and skill without fundamentally coding.

11.   Programming and application improvement

Need to take independent coding to a higher degree of business venture? Rather than assisting clients, you with canning work on your applications, projects, expansions, and additional items. Whether you sell your work in the App Store or bring in cash through ads — or you're waiting for the long stretch and are expecting to get purchased by a greater organization — the money you cause will be an immediate consequence of your work and creativity.

In contrast to normal outsourcing, however, this is somewhat of a harder nut to pop open. It's not as simple to have an anticipated stream of income until your application is now out and selling, and by then you've proactively invested a great deal of effort and energy. Hence, before you commit an outsourcing monetary error, you'll need to be certain that there's a market out there for the item you're making, and that individuals will pay for it.

All things considered, the successes can be huge. Might your task at some point be the following Minecraft or Angry Birds? Just a single method for finding out.

12. Photography
For those talented in photography, you should transform your energy into a check. Stock photograph destinations like Shutterstock and iStock will give you a commission on the photos you sell, so on the off chance that you're open to imparting your focal point to a great many others, this is a simple and helpful method for financing your opportunity.

Additionally, on the off chance that you're especially skilled, you should sell your photographs on additional select destinations with higher commission rates — or even your site or web store.

13. Business training
You'll require a decent history and different tributes to back you up, yet the business training industry is on the ascent — so this moment's the opportunity to participate. You can charge anyplace from under $100 to a few times that, contingent upon your qualifications and viability, and it's entirely OK to mentor via telephone or video talk rather than eye to eye.

So assuming you're keen on repairing different organizations and getting compensated for it, then, at that point, look at this web-based business thought.

14. School counseling
$40,000 for every course. That is how much some school mentors make, essentially by encouraging understudies and their families

on the most proficient method to make it into their fantasy schools.

While that is more the exemption than the standard, school counseling is a worthwhile business — and it tends to be finished via telephone or by video talk. You'll likely need to have gone to a top-level school yourself (to "demonstrate" to guardians that you know what you're talking about) and ought to have solid composing abilities, as school applications depend vigorously on private explanations and different expositions.

School counseling can incorporate monetary guide arranging too, and that implies you'll know about government award programs, different monetary guide strategies, and conceivable grant open doors.

15. Coaching
Assuming you're into online business thoughts for fledglings that rotate around calling or video talking clients to help them

out with different issues, then, at that point, beginning a mentoring business is one more way to consider.

For those diligent business visionaries who score exceptionally on state-sanctioned tests, comprehend how to show the best test-taking procedures, and know everything there is to know about their material, mentoring can pull in a huge load of cash without an excessive amount of exertion. The better your outcomes, the more prominent your standing — and that implies the more you can charge each hour, meeting, or bundle.

Also, with these internet-based independent venture thoughts — business training, school counseling, and coaching — you're committing your significant investment to assist others with accomplishing a portion of life's greatest objectives. Combined with the opportunity of working from any place you need, that is a really convincing position.

16. Online wellness mentor

"Online wellness preparing" could appear to be a paradoxical expression, yet it's a genuine industry — and on the off chance that you're putting resources into online business thoughts, don't ignore it.

If wellness and wellbeing are your obsession, filling in as a wellness coach to clients could be a satisfying vocation. Nonetheless, you ought to remember that preparing individuals online is significantly more troublesome than being not too far off with them. Without a great deal of involvement as a mentor, you could try and seem to be deceitful to likely clients.

There's consistently the chance for you to go to clients locally as opposed to maintaining an online business, however that probably won't be a good fit for you. Or on the other hand, you could balance your absence of an individual presents with a more grounded center around nourishment instruction.

17. Online business store
One of the most well-known internet-based business thoughts around, beginning a web-based business store is somewhat simple and modest — basically when contrasted with opening up a physical store.

Assuming you're convenient or inventive, you could create your items and sell them on locales like Etsy, Amazon, or eBay, straight out of your home. The greatest test would get found, contingent upon your specialty and how viral your items are. However, fortunately, there's lots of exhortation accessible to take care of you, from valuing your work appropriately to taking the most ideal photography.

18. Virtual secondhand store
Perhaps you're not into painstaking work but rather the possibility of an internet-based store is as yet engaging.

Online secondhand stores and transfer stores, such as thredUP, are one model you can follow to accomplish that objective. Different organizations slither through locales like eBay to track down cool, one-of-a-kind, fascinating items, then present them in convincing ways. Great copywriting and a solid brand can go quite far to isolating you from the group here.

So if you're more into organizing than making, these kinds of simple web-based business thoughts would be a strong fit.

19. Partner showcasing
Web-based entertainment masters, pay heed: you don't need to be an expert to profit from your person-to-person communication abilities.

All things considered, you can get compensated by organizations to feature items on your blog, Instagram, Twitter, YouTube, or other social channels. The higher your profile, the greater amount of the effect your image proposal will make, and the more you'll make with item situations. Since your fans aren't switched off by this promoting, partner, here and there alluded to as powerhouse showcasing is one method for utilizing your web-based entertainment abilities to your advantage.

Furthermore, similar to the remainder of these internet-based business thoughts, you can be a partner advertiser from any place you need, with the opportunity and adaptability to pick your hours and work for yourself.

20. Web space selling

Managing in web spaces is like trading land — except you can do it from your PC at home. Here is the abominable: some web space names are more famous, pursued, and significant than others. Effective web space name flippers purchase high-esteem spaces for inexpensive online closeouts after heaps of planning and exploration, then offer them to the greatest bidder for a decent benefit. For instance, www.hotels.com was sold for $11 million in 2001.

To get by off of space selling, you truly need to commit your time, energy, and thoughtfulness regarding the market. You can't simply purchase space names haphazardly, or you'll be left with a small bunch of sites that no one needs. All things considered, you'll need to investigate the SEO streamlining of the destinations you see up for sale, anticipate which organizations and businesses will be paying special attention to new areas, and get imaginative with out-of-the-container names that you can purchase for close to nothing yet pivot without any problem. Besides, persistence is an ethicalness: it can require months, or even years, to get the right cost for certain spaces you've bought.

Yet, the advantage of this web-based business thought, is that it's 100 percent on the web. It's simply you and your PC.

21. Bookkeeping or accounting
Even though entering the business as a virtual clerk or bookkeeper can be intense in light of rivalry from unfamiliar project workers, some firms offer these administrations. You likewise could take your ongoing clients, on the off chance that you're as of now working as a bookkeeper, and propose to reduce their expenses by telecommuting or remotely somewhere else.

Normally, online business thoughts like these require formal preparation and certificate, however, if you're a demonstrated and committed bookkeeper, it ought not to be difficult to work online the vast majority of the time.

22. Selling

On the off chance that you're a characteristic conversationalist who preferences helping other people, virtual selling is one more great web-based independent company thought to consider. A lot of organizations reevaluate a portion of their deals and client care staff, so if you wouldn't fret working the telephone at home or in a hurry, then, at that point, give this choice a shot.

23. Online individual partner
Coordinated. Productive. Hungry to carry on with life on your timetable?

On the off chance that those three things depict you, contemplate turning into a menial helper. What precisely you'll do relies upon what your abilities, experience, and organization of contacts are, however you can anticipate that undertakings from information passage should client the board, examination, planning and that's only the tip of the iceberg. What's more, obviously, similar to all web-based business thoughts, you can do this one from any place.

24. Information passage

Even though it doesn't pay the best, the information section is an internet-based business thought where you can undoubtedly telecommute. If you're searching for a task that will not call for much investment or consideration from you, and that you can make unsurprising pay from while at home or voyaging, then information passage is a decent spot to begin.

25. Stock or unfamiliar cash exchanging

Like web space name selling, stock exchange could be a relaxed internet-based side interest or a vocation. On the off chance that you're willing to invest the energy and you're capable of doing profound exploration and foreseeing patterns, you could transform this side gig into a full-time gig.

Working as an example informal investor expects you to keep $25,000 in your record consistently, however, so if that obstruction to passage is all too high, you should consider exchanging on unfamiliar trade or money markets all things being equal.

Everything that is expressed, stock exchanging won't offer you as much adaptability as large numbers of the other web-based business thoughts here. Even though you can telecommute and work for yourself assuming that you exchange stocks or unfamiliar cash on your dime, it's as yet a high-responsibility work with extended periods and a lofty expectation to learn and adapt. You'll have to invest the effort to see all the different exchanging prerequisites, frameworks, and guidelines you'll interface with.

26. Record
For a simpler web-based business thought that doesn't need foundation information or

experience — other than the capacity to type rapidly — you should seriously mull over the record. Offering record administrations online can take many structures: you can translate sound meetings for columnists, make subtitles for TV shows and recordings or foster deciphered adaptations of digital broadcasts.

Albeit this probably won't be the most worthwhile thought on our rundown, it's a decent spot to begin as a specialist and allows you to work any place, at whatever point.

27. Travel arranging

Do you very much want to travel? Have you been to different areas and have an organization of associations all over the planet? Assuming that movement is your obsession, you should seriously think about beginning an internet-based travel arranging business. You can assist clients with arranging each part of their outing —

from trips to lodgings to activities. You can deal with schedules, tips for food, money trade, and security, and act as a resource between your clients and any global contacts.

Additionally, besides the fact that you work can your movement arranging business at home, yet you can likewise do it while you travel. Furthermore, voyaging will assist you with developing your business — as you experience new areas, meet planned clients, and make new associations. You could try and begin a sightseeing web journal or photography webpage to enhance your arranging business.

28. Network safety and IT counseling
If you have a specialized foundation yet aren't explicitly keen on coding or application improvement, this may be one of the most mind-blowing web-based business thoughts for you. As a network protection expert, you can work with

organizations, everything being equal, to assess their frameworks, run testing and deal tips on how they can work on their setup.

Then again, on the off chance that you'd favor something more extensive, you should seriously think about basically filling in as an IT advisor, helping organizations or people with their innovation — assisting them with getting it set up, investigating any issues, and dealing general working exhortation.

Indeed, with the appropriate PC setup, you can run your network safety or IT counseling business from any place. If you so decide, you could likewise choose to venture out to various workplaces for periodic on-location framework help.

29. Online treatment
With the rise of organizations like TalkSpace and BetterHelp, you never again must have

an office or your training to advise patients — you can do it. Albeit this web-based business thought requires legitimate certifications and instruction, an innovatively slanted specialist who needs to arrive at another gathering of patients could without much of a stretch set it all up.

On the off chance that you're an instructor, specialist, or clinician, you could choose to investigate the internet-based treatment space by going along with one of these new organizations or beginning your very own business. By directing on the web, you'll arrive at new patients, giving them more opportunity and adaptability, as well as partaking in some for yourself.

30. PR counseling
Assuming you're knowledgeable about business marking and advertising and know the very most effective ways for organizations to speak with the public on the web, you could begin an internet-based

PR counseling business. You can help organizations with their internet-based presence — including virtual entertainment accounts, official statements, and web content from there, the sky is the limit — as well as exhort them on missions, drives, and by and large open picture.

As an independent PR expert, your hours and obligations might differ and rely upon the particular client you're working with, be that as it may, you'll surely have more control of your occupation than you would as a feature of a PR firm or organization.

31. Podcasting

A decade prior, many individuals didn't have the foggiest idea what a web recording was nevertheless now, the digital broadcast industry has detonated, with papers, radio broadcasts, and, surprisingly, customary, regular people getting in on the pattern. On the off chance that you have a decent story to tell or something you feel like you could discuss on a successive premise and that individuals would need to pay attention to, you could ponder podcasting.

Podcasting should be possible from any place, given you have the right sound hardware. You can then transfer your substance to different webcast applications, and sites, and market your business via virtual entertainment.

32. Life training

Searching for the thing on this rundown of online private venture thoughts that permits you to help individuals, offering both exhortation and direction, without requiring the broad schooling of a clinical expert? Could life training? Even though you might require confirmation to turn into a holistic mentor, you have substantially more opportunity to track down your specialty and conclude how you can assist with peopling through life's promising and less promising times.

Besides, as a holistic mentor, you can fabricate your computerized image to give your clients extra assets beyond the customary call or video talk gatherings. With the immeasurability of the web readily available, you can undoubtedly satisfy your craving to help other people with this internet-based business thought, while as yet having the adaptability of your own.

33. Video creation

Video is one more thing on our rundown of online business thoughts that might speak to you, particularly assuming that you're imaginative or know quite a bit about computerized creation. With the accentuation on record on social media and different sites these days, this is unquestionably a pattern you'll need to profit by while you can. This being said, as a video maker, you can work with various clients in different enterprises to shoot, slice, and alter videos to make the ideal eventual outcome.

Even though video creation can be on the specialized side, it likewise can offer you the chance to investigate a one-of-a-kind mechanism of narrating and practice your imagination. Furthermore, if you don't as of now have video experience, there are numerous assets accessible online to show you and help you through the cycle.

34. Computerized publicizing

Could it be said that you know about the universe of "cost per click" and the always-changing Facebook calculation? If you have insight into the inward activities of promoting on the web — from sites to virtual entertainment stages to email crusades — you should seriously think about beginning this internet-based business thought from home.

As a computerized promoting specialist, clients could enlist you to adapt their web-based stages and deal with the entire publicizing efforts. Albeit this space is continually advancing, it has dynamically become increasingly more critical to organizations, particularly those that chiefly work on the web. You can offer your promoting mastery from any place and work with clients only using email or telephone.

35. Continue composing and professional training

On the off chance that you have experience with HR, or simply feel comfortable around planning the ideal resume, you should think about beginning a web-based continue composing and profession instructing business. You can offer clients exhortation and direction on their vocation way, requests for employment continues, and introductory letters. LinkedIn is an incredible spot to get everything rolling with this kind of internet-based business thought, as numerous experts search for professional help on that stage.

Also, the entirety of your to and fro with clients should be possible by talk, email, or telephone — enabling you to work any place and pick your hours.

36. Outsourcing

On the off chance that you don't need the obligation of making your items to sell, you should seriously mull over rather beginning an outsourcing business. With this sort of internet business activity, you can pick items from providers and afterward sell them on the web. You can make your site, assemble your interaction and direct all aspects of your web-based business.

You can begin by perusing outsourcing commercial centers or attempting to work straightforwardly with producers and merchants. As web-based business keeps on developing, there will be no lack of chances in the outsourcing space.

37. Web-based selecting
Have a skill for tracking down the perfect individuals to fill employment opportunities? If you're an extrovert and have great web-based research abilities, you should seriously mull over this work on our rundown of online private company thoughts: selecting. As a web-based scout, you would support various organizations hoping to enlist new representatives and help them find and screen applicants.

As an incredible piece of the enrolling system for organizations has become online-based, there will be no deficiency of need for this sort of administration, particularly for more modest organizations that don't have a huge HR group or the assets and time to appropriately commit to selecting.

38. Promoting counseling
Promoting is workmanship and on the off chance that you have abilities or involvement in any sort of showcasing efforts, you should seriously mull over offering counseling administrations as a web-based business. As a showcasing specialist, you can give direction on a great many subjects, contingent upon your particular mastery, and assist organizations with executing their promoting techniques and missions.

From email promoting techniques to occasion intending to site marking, organizations will continuously have advertising needs and your web-based business can be there to help.

39. Web-based raising money or award composing
Do you have a reason you're energetic? Or on the other hand, perhaps you're only energetic about aiding mission-based

organizations, particularly non-benefits, getting the help they need to arrive at their objectives. If both of these situations concern you, you ought to ponder raising support or award composing as a business. With these web-based attempts, you would work with clients who need assistance with their gathering pledges crusades — tracking down planned contributors, advancing the business and their objectives, and, eventually, attempting to acquire reserves.

Or on the other hand, if you need to reach out past one individual to another gathering pledges, you could work with clients to explore and compose award applications and attempt to get them the assets they need in like that.

40. Online course instructing
Is there a subject you're especially learned about? American history? Tax documents? Drawing? On the off chance that you have a camera and a PC, you could begin an

internet-based course educating business. You can track down data about essentially anything on the web, yet some of the time while you're attempting to get familiar with particular expertise or subject, it simply assists with hearing or seeing another person make sense of it. Your course-showing business would exploit this need, offering instructive support to your specific crowd.

In addition, assuming you have a postgraduate education or showing foundation, you could work with a web-based course administration, that will recruit you to show courses online for their understudies.

41. Web-based cooking guidance
Do you have a fondness for cooking or baking? Exhibiting your abilities online using virtual cooking classes is an incredible method for bringing in cash while accomplishing something you love. There

are different ways you can structure your cooking business — you can offer one-on-one guidance recordings, have live classes, and even make studios and cooking programs.

This simple business thought really might convert into a cooking blog, digital books, cookbooks, and connecting your #1 cooking and baking supplies through partner showcasing.

42. YouTube channel
On the off chance that you're enthusiastic about a subject, possibly a specialty and perusers are searching for the substance you need to share. One method for advancing your new image, administration, or message is by making a YouTube channel. On the off chance that you feel great on camera, have where you can film, and want to arrive at millions on the web, YouTube may be the right stage for you.

It can require an investment for your channel to develop and you'll probably have to organize via online entertainment and publishing content to a blog stage at the outset, yet with commitment, you can make an open to living along these lines.

43. Voiceover work

Assuming you're searching for an internet-based business thought that you can begin from home, rapidly and effectively, you could choose to begin your own voiceover business. All you want is a good receiver, essential sound-altering programming, and the capacity to loan your voice to promotional firms, creation organizations, and any other person searching for a voiceover.

To begin, you can pursue an independent voiceover site like Voices.com and begin looking for the perfect times. Additionally, whenever you've secured your opportunity, you'll have astounding clasps to show expected future clients.

44. Begin a group

On the off chance that you've been outsourcing or running your organization for some time, you may be prepared to go all in and begin your group of advisors, consultants, specialists, and so on.

For example, if you have long periods of composing and altering experience and find new clients rapidly, you should build the number of chances you can take by employing a group of consultants to assist with developing your business.

The reality

By the day's end, these web-based business thoughts aren't the only ways of getting away from the workplace way of life. All things considered, they offer a sort of opportunity that a great many people don't have the potential chance to encounter:

overseeing yourself, making your schedule and objectives, and getting a sense of ownership with your work in the most significant manner. This being said, albeit beginning an internet-based business might give you remarkable adaptability, it likewise implies endeavoring to track down clients, market your administration and keep up with consistent income.

Blueline Business Checking
Blueline Business Checking
NerdWallet rating
at Blueline, Deposits are FDIC Insured

Online organizations aren't ideal for everybody. Assuming you're thinking about any of the things on this rundown of online business thoughts for fledglings, however, there could be no greater opportunity to get everything rolling. By investigating the various potential outcomes, finding a startup thought that will work for you, exploring quite a bit early, and executing a compelling field-tested strategy, you'll be headed to a fruitful way of life that the vast majority just dream about.

www.ingramcontent.com/pod-product-compliance
Lightning Source LLC
Chambersburg PA
CBHW071456150726
48000CB00006B/2592